A Conversation with Ambassador
Tahseen Basheer

American Enterprise Institute
Studies in Foreign Policy

Ambassador

Tahseen Basheer

Reflections on the Middle East Peace Process

A Conversation with Ambassador

Tahseen Basheer

Reflections on the Middle East Peace Process

Held on April 2, 1981
at the American Enterprise Institute for Public Policy Research
Washington, D.C.

ISBN 0–8447–3469–1

Library of Congress Catalog Card No. 81–69953

AEI Studies 342

Printed in the United States of America

Introduction

Ambassador Tahseen Basheer, Egypt's ambassador-designate to Canada, has always been an active member of the Egyptian foreign ministry. He has served as supervisor of presidential press affairs for President Anwar Sadat, as Egypt's spokesman at the peace talks from 1973 to 1975, as ambassador to the Arab League, and as a delegate to the United Nations. He has also been a resident fellow at the American Enterprise Institute for several months.

The role Egypt has played in the peace process and the subsequent benefit of close U.S.–Egyptian relations make the Egyptian view particularly pertinent at a time when the Reagan administration is in the process of fashioning a policy on the Middle East. This discussion with Ambassador Basheer, like the discussions we have had with others and will continue to have in the near future, provides a unique opportunity to hear and debate many perspectives on the Middle East, an area so central for U.S. foreign policy.

JUDITH KIPPER
American Enterprise Institute

A Conversation with Ambassador Tahseen Basheer

It is not from lack of modesty that I dare tackle the subject of peace in the Middle East. It is instead that I have lived so long with this tragedy, both at home and in a personal sense. I am encouraged by the fact that everybody who tries to help, who lights one candle and fails to light a big light, is in good company. For the last thirty years, despite continuous efforts to solve the Middle East peace problem, it has eluded solution. We have turned to chapter six of the United Nations Charter, with all its enumeration of specific ways to settle problems, and yet we have only the start of a peace process.

We must remember what the peace process today is all about. We face a historical tragedy that produced multiple promises. It is a tragedy the Arabs, particularly the Palestinians, who did not understand why an innocent people should lose their land and become homeless, lose their political sovereignty and be denied recognition even by a superpower that champions freedom. It is a tragedy that Jews who sought their promised land after the holocausts and their own haven of self-employment had to encroach upon basically innocent people.

The crucial proposal which agreed in 1947 and 1948 to partition failed to ensure that the partition would be peaceful and that all the arguments and assurances in the partition plan would be respected. In fact, it seems an added tragedy to have expected the Arabs, and particularly the Arabs of Palestine, to accept voluntarily the partition of their country.

What we witnessed or experienced between 1948 and 1977 was the creation and solidification of a vicious circle. The participants were partly innocent, partly not—like everything human, it is ambivalent. The relationship between Jews, who created a country in Israel, and the Arabs around them became what strategists call a zero-sum dispute. Professor Talmon of Hebrew University distilled the essence of the tragedy when he said that the Arab and Israeli conflict is like an immovable object and an irresistible force of hate and disagreement. Though Professor Talmon believed in peace, he did not see how that peace would come about. The situation became a zero-sum conflict in which every benefit that might come to one side was seen by the other as equally injurious to it, and for almost thirty years we had no solution.

Each side tried to improve its position with respect to the other through a political system having two tightly knit constituencies—an Arab constituency and an Israeli constituency. Within each of these constituencies were many—sometimes conflicting—subdivisions, but basically they agreed, in a de facto way, to keep the conflict alive. Superpowers, such as the United States, Europe, and the United Nations, for thirty years offered only minor, aspirin-type solutions to some problems.

By the early 1950s, all the superpowers had given up the idea of a global solution to this problem. That status quo became entrenched, and no matter what other changes took place in the Middle East, that status quo continued to exist, in peace and in war.

During that time, no one offered alternatives. The real alternatives that would work were what one side wanted the other to submerge in different formulas. One would call it a Palestinian secular state, the other would call it the unification of the East Bank and the West Bank, but the end result was that the Palestinian side disappeared. The other technique on each side was delay ad infinitum. Under the British mandate, the Israelis said the Arabs were not ready for democracy. The Palestinians would not answer *the* question. They said, "There is a suitable saying for every situation." In Arabic, for each situation, there is a saying—there is always another time, another place.

During that period, there was no possibility of compromise. Aside from a few margins here and there, the argument used by either side was all or nothing. Compromise was seen as betrayal, sometimes crudely expressed, sometimes more subtly. Also during that time, both sides, in varying degrees at various times, played certain games. Let me give you a taste of these games.

First, each side maintained, "The burden of proof is on you, not on me. You have to prove your good intentions, not I." The second game was that each acted as a mirror image of the other. In 1942, an armed Mr. Begin was happy to claim he was a terrorist, and he was able to fight the British. The Israelis called it a war of independence, an anticolonial war. The Palestinians today call it a war of national liberation.

4

Each side also played another game—the double agenda, or double-talk. At no time did each put on the table, clearly and honestly, the real double agenda—what is intended and what is said. The fourth game was using tension as a means of political mobilization and of nation building. Both sides had nations that were reborn or just born, and they needed some tension to manipulate their constituents.

The fifth game was to appeal to a third party. The third party differs—the United States, the West, the Third World, the United Nations—any third party. The Arabs for a long time thought that if America knew the truth, it will be just and fair. Israel also appealed very strongly to America to be its underwriter and supporter. Also, third parties were equally blamed when things went sour. The sixth game they played is that each side claimed the force of history on its side, so, given time, each would succeed.

The most important game, the seventh, was each side never accepted the other on the other's own terms. The Arabs wanted deZionization. The Israelis want to neutralize the Arabs. The Arabs as a group would not accept it, although there are moderate Arabs who accept Israel. In the meantime, an eighth game developed, and that was tragic. Each side victimized the other, dehumanized it, and instead of having a dialogue, we have had continuous monologues, mostly directed at the believers and the people on the periphery watching the feud escalate.

The ninth game was played by the superpowers. The superpowers particularly have shown either a lack of interest in a global settlement or an impotence to achieve that settlement. The two main superpowers supported the partition, but they have failed to work together to bring about a stable and meaningful peace.

Like all political controversies this one has a cost, and for the last thirty years, the constituents paid the cost of keeping the status quo of war. In human political terms, we, the partners to that conflict, paid it, but in monetary terms, in arms terms, it was financed by outside powers.

What started as a tragedy has become a vicious circle.

When did the change happen? Two factors brought it about. One is a number of events I will call negative changes. The first change was the total defeat of the Arabs in the war of 1967. With this defeat, Israel achieved maximum military success, but it also achieved total political failure. Israel, which now controlled all of the Palestinians, particularly those within the boundaries of Palestine, plus the Golan and Sinai, failed up until 1973 to bring about one new idea for settling the Palestinian issue, either the political issue of the refugees or the integration of Palestinians into any body that exists in the Middle East, even if it is Jordan. There was no novelty in the way Israel continued the conflict after its total military success. In fact, the war of 1973 was born out of Israeli political failure since 1967.

The second element of negative change was silent change. For the first time, Egypt and the rest of the Arab world, in varying degrees, conducted an internal dialogue, mostly in silence, trying to face up to the peace problem—what to do with it. Are we and our children and generations to come going to live our lives in unending war? That dialogue, which was not expressed publicly until later, was one of the basic elements that changed the status quo.

The third change was the political national regeneration of the Palestinians, a revolt against Arab government policies with respect to the Palestinians and the Israeli occupation. The Palestinian people felt they needed self-reliance. They cannot depend on other Arabs, they cannot depend on the superpowers, and they cannot depend on Israeli intentions. Their national regeneration became a fact, an indelible fact.

The fourth factor was the change in the role of the superpowers. They became captives of the status quo. They financed the status quo, they invested in the status quo, but they were never able to change it. We have had an escalation of the arms transfer. The latest techniques and arms were used in the war of 1973, but it did not solve the basic problem.

The positive change did not come about until President Sadat visited Jerusalem and talked to the Israelis sensibly and sensitively, trying to understand their wants and at the same time acquainting them with Arab concerns and asking them to help heal Arab wounds. Only then, for the first time, did the vicious circle start to be broken. It was the first time since this conflict started, since the 1917 mandate and the Balfour Declaration, that we had a change of scenario from a zero-sum to a non-zero-sum game. Since that time, we have had possibilities for mutual development of varying degrees, and because of that, we have had what is now called the peace process.

We have now had peace between Egypt and Israel for almost two years. What are some of the results of that peace? I will be very candid with you about these results, because in peace one has to face all the limitations of the process to be able to surmount them and move ahead. First, the peace process means no return to the previous status quo. No matter what will happen in the short run, no matter what the fluctuations—one step backward, two steps backward, one step forward, two steps forward—the secular trend in the peace relationship will never allow a return to the status quo ante between Egypt and Israel, nor between the Arabs and Israel.

Second, the Arab-Israeli confrontation is not the same. For the first time, Israel does not face a realistic, major Arab attack. That has become something of the past. That does not mean that we do not have forays of fighting now and then or that we do not have other tensions, such as that in Lebanon, but a major war is out.

Third, the positions of the parties are undergoing radical change and will undergo further radical change. After a period of adjustment, no matter who attempts to keep the old position, it becomes expensive and difficult to keep the status quo. We have to move ahead; we cannot go back. This is one of the dilemmas the parties face.

The fourth result of the peace process is that constituencies have changed. In the Arab constituency, even those states that opted to suspend Egyptian membership in the Arab League and the Islamic Conference have moderated their positions. All the efforts by some of the extreme rejectionists to change the trend of Arab policy toward peace has failed. Despite the Arab rejection of the peace process of Camp David and the peace treaty, the Arab trend toward peace has continued. Prince Fahd last year admitted the possibility of recognition of Israel by Saudi Arabia. The Israeli attitudes have also changed. Prominent among them is the rise of a new constituency of young Israeli men and women in a peace-now movement across all political frontiers. But all Israelis, regardless of political posture, are trying to grope with this problem.

The fifth element of change was the break in the status quo. That break has ushered in a sensitive, almost dangerous, period of dynamic change. This is the period we are in. It has a negative aspect, which is the possibility of destructive activities in response to the insecurity of that change. The Arabs, for example, feel they have lost their big brother, Egypt, and do not have that shoulder to rely on. The Begin government in Israel feels that because Egypt is involved in withdrawal from Sinai, they might try to attack Southern Lebanon or further escalate their attacks on the Palestinians. So there has been a negative, destructive aspect of this new dynamic change, but the positive aspect is very clear. For the first time, we have genuine, organic opportunities to develop the peace process on a mutually agreed-upon basis.

The sixth element in the peace process, which is very important and much neglected, is the element of self-reliance. When Sadat went to Jerusalem—surprising not only the enemy of yesterday,

Israel, but his friends the Americans as well—he demonstrated an element of self-reliance. Small and medium-sized powers must share responsibility for themselves. They cannot rely on superpowers to hand them the solution to their problems on a platter. Mr. Begin, in accepting the removal of Israeli settlements from Sinai, realized that it is in the interests of his own constituency to move, even in a limited sense, the process of peace. The role of third parties—the United States or the Soviet Union or Europe—is important. It is important as an encourager of the process, but I feel that a genuine process of peace will have to rely in the long term on the self-reliance of the primary parties. They, and they alone, can break through what seems impossible.

The seventh factor has been the creation of a new center of stability in the Middle East—Egypt and Israel. We have a lot of differences with each other, but a center of stability is there. It also is breeding in the Middle East the possibility of a new parallel co-operation, a cooperation that is not enunciated in so many words but is evident in the rationality of the interests of the parties. That is turning over a new page in the Middle East. Now, here are some other results from the peace process. One is that the whole future of the Middle East seems to be in a process of remolding. You find people talking about Palestinian states, or a federation, or a Jordanian-Palestinian state like the one the labor party of Israel has included in its own political platform. The whole Middle East is undergoing a process, like the process after the First World War, of remolding. Second, the old arguments of each of the parties are losing their strength. The same threats are being invoked every day, but they do not have the same echo. Third, there has been an attempt to arrest the change. There has been a change in rhetoric without changing the content.

The fourth element is very important. Both parties are now seeing their dilemmas more clearly than before. There are an Arab dilemma and an Israeli dilemma, and I will explain them in a little while. The fifth element is that considerations in the Middle East— the oil boom, the fantastic wealth, the security of the area, the Russian threat, the threat from forces within the area, whether it is radicalism of Islam or radicalism of the rest of the left—all these parameters are putting the Arab-Israeli conflict in a different light.

The sixth element is a change in the perception of timing. The present seems to be more important to many people in the Middle East than the past, or the continuation of the past. The future tends to carry the present rather than the past, and that is a new orientation. Many people in the Middle East have lived as if life is a continuum of museum life. Now, the people in the Middle East are seeing their lives as something new, a new challenge and a new life.

The seventh element of change is that Egypt and Israel have not only learned to agree but, more important, they have also learned to disagree. We have disagreed a lot with Israel without going to verbal wars or real wars. We have agreed on many things and we have disagreed, but we have agreed to contain our disagreements in a way conducive to building peace. From the Egyptian point of view, Israel has at least two major constituencies. One is the Israeli government, and, like any government, it is a question of convenience. But we face a much more important constitutency in the Israeli people. Peace, to us, means the creation of a constituency, not Arab versus Israeli, but a new constituency in the Middle East that includes both Arabs and Israelis for a reasonable, effective peace—that is, Arabs and Israelis who expect a gradual, effective peace.

The eighth element we face in this process is normalization. Israelis come to Egypt en masse, and of late they have been a little bit surprised by the fact that they are taken for granted. Egyptians are not surprised when they see Israelis, and some Israelis do not feel comfortable with that. Some Israelis are critical of the process of normalization. They want forced normalization. "Forced" and "normalization" are mutually exclusive terms. There can be no real normalization while the Egyptians feel the Palestinians are mistreated. Our normalization must take a realistic view of the fact that we are in the beginning of the peace process and not at the end.

About the dilemmas, there are three: an Israeli-Jewish dilemma, an Arab dilemma, and the peace dilemma.

I cannot say much about the Israeli-Jewish dilemma. I would rather leave it to the Israelis and to the Jewish community all over the world to discuss whether the original formula of Zionism—that the only solution to this huge problem is the gathering of all the Jews—will be a realistic, healthy formula for Jewish liberation and fulfillment. The fact is, with Israel achieving statehood and a degree of prosperity, the majority of the Jews in the Western countries have opted not to go to Israel. They support Israel financially and politically, and they are committed to the new state, but the Zionist formula has not fulfilled itself and there is a dilemma to be faced.

The Israeli dilemma that concerns me most is best illustrated by the two major political parties in Israel. The territorialists of Mr. Begin—Likud and Herut—want to keep all the land. They want to have military power for the time being to keep all of the West Bank and Gaza. If they do so, however, they will create a binational state, a territory that in ten or twenty years will have an equivalent number of Jews and Arabs and will be multinational, multireligious, and multilingual. If the Zionist movement ends up under good enough leadership to produce a pluralistic system in Israel, then what was the Zionist movement all about? Pluralism has been much better fulfilled in New York state, elsewhere in the United States, or in other Western countries. If the Zionist movement keeps faithful to its tenets, then the act of territorial acquisition is a self-defeating act in Zionist terms.

The second half of this dilemma is the Labor Party proposal for partition—give the Arabs all the Arabic-inhabited areas, and take all other land. This kind of partition tends to say we do not want Arabs, but we will take all the land that might give them life. It kills the possibility of Arab life, though it leaves the Arabs or sends them back to Jordan.

These two positions are the basic dilemma in dealing with the Palestinian problem. That is why we have a whole parade of diplomatic techniques, trying to ward off facing the real problem. We have the Jordanian option, we have Mr. Dayan's unilateral autonomy, we have autonomy, we have concerts of condominium, we have concerts of federation, conference systems, functional autonomy, and all of that. All these policies offer us form but have very little content, because they do not answer the question how to resolve the Palestinian problem.

We also have an Arab-Palestinian dilemma. The Palestinian dilemma is very difficult because the new reality is that 3 million or more Israelis live in 80 percent, or almost 80 percent, of what the Palestinians historically regarded as their country. Many of these Israelis are innocent of the question of who created what in which year with what legality. They were born there, and they will fight to retain their rights. Palestinians then have to face the dilemma of accepting that the best they can do is to create a state to express their self-determination in a small part of their country, the West Bank and Gaza. That is a difficult dilemma; they must face it and accept it without a double agenda of irredentism. Just as the Israelis must face their dilemma without reverting back to the Israel the Bible mapped out, the Arabs also face a dilemma because the Palestinian population that exists in Lebanon and in the Persian Gulf states—Kuwait particularly—once the political problem has been solved must be integrated into the body Arab, in one form or another. Support for the Palestinians becomes not simply the test of voting for Palestinian issues in the United Nations or of giving money and arms to the Palestinian Liberation Organization (the PLO) it becomes acceptance of the Palestinian people as citizens in body Arab. This

10

Arab-Palestinian dilemma is very crucial, and so far many Arabs have many answers, but they have not faced that dilemma squarely and fairly.

To illustrate the peace dilemma, let me start with a simple proposition. Within the context of the Israelis keeping the security of the West Bank and Gaza, Israel never offered any proposal to grant the Palestinians their full civil, economic, and political rights. Even though the Israeli army offers them security, Israel failed to offer a political settlement to this issue.

The peace dilemma is difficult, and it has many levels. First, we have a conceptual dilemma. Some people think peace is a deal to maintain a normal relationship between one country and another. There is also the concept of peace as real revolution, the only revolution in the Middle East that affects the long-term interests of the mass of people. They have been the fodder of war; they paid for war; now peace in the long run will go to their benefit. This concept of peace as a revolution has not been accepted. It is a peaceful revolution, not so noisy, but very effective. Peace is structural change like that in Europe after the Second World War, when there was a whole recreation of a new Europe. In my opinion, there will be no persistent peace unless there is a basic structural change in the Middle East.

These two competing concepts—peace as a deal between two countries versus peace as a structural revolutionary change—bring about the second problem in the peace dilemma, the bargaining problem. Some Arabs and some Israelis feel the bargaining is like bazaar bargaining, tit for tat, but a multiple, complex kind of tit for tat. Because of the time dimension, the tits and tats are not comparable, so we face instead the other kind of bargaining, the bargaining for building a new structure rather than tit for tat. I do not think the bazaar-type arrangement, though needed, is the key to that structure. Instead, a more complex, multifaceted bargaining must take place.

A third problem is the diplomatic games both sides play. We have several diplomatic games: the fragmentation of the problem; the changing language of UN Resolution 242; the Geneva Conference versus bilateral talks. Then we have the game of musical chairs. Who are the parties to the negotiations? Who are the surrogates? One delegation or many? Another game is to say the PLO no, the Palestinians okay. But then how do you represent the Palestinians? Is anybody today willing to have a process of self-determination by the Palestinians? Those who attack the PLO have not offered an alternative of going directly to the Palestinian people.

Another problem in the peace dilemma is the Palestinian autonomy negotiations. I can summarize the autonomy negotiations, which took about twenty-one months, as an attempt by the Begin government to make a unilateral Israeli change in the status quo. It hoped to change the status quo contrary to the peace treaty at Camp David in order to radicalize the Palestinians and make them not qualified to enter the negotiating team. We have seen Israel attempt to change the demographic composition, the geographic character, and the legal status of the West Bank and Gaza. We have seen policies that tend to contribute to an atmosphere conducive to making the Palestinians of the West Bank and Gaza lose faith in the peace process and alienate themselves from it.

After twenty-one months, the negotiation ended in a knot—there has been no progress. The only progress was that we and the Israelis have exhibited a lot of patience, a lot of self-control, and an ability to pin down the problems. I should add that I am not particularly impressed by the creative power of the third party—that is, the United States—in the autonomy negotiations. The United States should have played a much more active, dynamic role instead of trying to pat each side on the back and to avoid facing difficult problems.

With that, I go to the real issues, because we do face real issues. The first issue is that the Camp David process of reaching a peace treaty is not sacrosanct. It is a process capable of development, modification, addition, and change. Camp David was created out of a deadlock, a deadlock that could have been continued by President Sadat saying no to President Carter. Instead, President Sadat took the risk of peace, and because he took the risk of peace, this process evolved and became legal. But any change, modification, and addition should come about with prior consultation among the parties. Also, we must underline the obligations in the peace treaty and in the Camp David meetings. We should build on these obligations and not accept any red herrings that will minimize or belittle the basic achievements.

There is no best formula developed yet. The best formula so far is the not-so-best formula we have at hand. It has a lot of limitations, but whatever formula evolves must have two or three factors that are essential to the peace process. One is the transitional period. Two is that all the parties, including the Palestinian people, must fully participate in the final settlement. Three, there should be no unilateral change in the status quo, and there should be no cheating.

The second important issue is the failure of the rejectionists, both Arab and Israeli, to offer an alternative. This amounts to a veto power over progress, because the Arab coalition and the Israeli co-

12

alition depend on small but extremist elements. Solving this problem depends on our ability to break the vicious circles of coalition and to limit the veto power of both sides.

The third real issue we face is delineated by two choices. One, in negotiating we have to agree on the shape of a global settlement. Then, the parties must negotiate the minutest details of its implementation in stages. But at least the parties will have an image of what lies at the end of the tunnel. The second choice is a process that started and concluded at Camp David—that is, agreeing on a process of negotiation that, at best, results in the principal points of agreement for a sequel to this stage of negotiation.

The fourth issue, timing, is very important in this process. It must be now. The parties must not be allowed to delay ad infinitum playing the game of deferral. Also, no one party should decide who will play the game. All the parties, including the Palestinians who have been excluded from official meetings with the American government representatives (that is, the PLO) should be invited to the peace negotiations. If you want to invite them, however, you have to accept a system of self-determination for the mass of the Palestinian people.

The fifth issue is that we need real, not make-believe, solutions. Many people offer solutions that have no content, while what is needed is to face the difficult questions. To do that and to accept peace as a real revolution, we must accept the following propositions: (1) Each side must accept the other as that side defines itself, and each side must face its own dilemmas; (2) each side must meet the minimum political requirements, the minimum concerns on the other side; (3) each side must negate the factors that tend to give a perception of real threat to the other; (4) it is very important to encourage and invest in the healing process; and (5) the new constituency of Arabs and Israelis for real peace must be encouraged to become eventually the strongest, overriding constituency in the Middle East.

Let me conclude with some prospects. I am not a believer in crystal balls, but I believe that the future has some prospects we can identify.

One prospect is the increased element of risk between now and the end of the Israeli elections. In fact, as soon as the secretary of state declares he will visit the area, some groups try to assert their prowess over the others—trying to make a point. Between now and the Israeli election is a very sensitive period because we do not know what each side will do to influence the outcome of the elections. There has been an escalation in Southern Lebanon, in the attempt to create faits accomplis, that is against the Camp David agreement.

Also, the Middle East lacks a shock absorber. The Iran-Iraq War has tended to absorb some of the Arab attention, and there is no way to allay fears during that time. We need a sustained effort to undergo this period peacefully.

A second prospect is the silent majority—a consensus that nobody talks about. There is in Israel a consensus not to expel or kill the Palestinians. The political parties and their constituencies say no return to June 5th borders, no Palestinian state between Israel and Jordan. But nobody talks about the other consensus, that the Palestinians cannot be killed, expelled, or pushed out. It is this constituency that we must develop and help to evolve and translate into political terms. There is also an Arab silent majority. The Arab silent majority wants peace, and it sees a lot of the affluence that comes with the oil boom not going to the people and not going into the desert to the Arabs but going to the very few. They want this historical boon to be of benefit to the area.

Another important prospect is that the cost of keeping the now-changed, unsettled status quo is very expensive. Neither the United States nor Saudi Arabia can finance this very unsettled status quo. The political and economic dimensions of the arms race are tremendous, and this status quo has become counterproductive in terms of inflation, capital, and incomes of the people involved.

A fourth prospect is that, for the time, we have bigger trade-offs. In the past, the Arabs and the Israelis were takers; they wanted handouts. Who would have thought twenty-five or thirty years ago that Saudi Arabia would be that rich? Now, it is among the richest countries in the world. Before, the superpowers gave and the Arabs took, that superpower gave and Israel took. Now, the Arabs have offered trade-offs much bigger than the small, limited confines of Palestine and Israel.

Israel, which has a psychological problem recognized in the peace treaty by Egypt, has now recognized a new peace process ushered in by Egypt. Egypt has been the innovator of peace, but Egypt cannot offer bridges of acceptance to Israel. We must distinguish between recognition and acceptance. Acceptance means accepting the other side on its own terms as part of the area, accepting it on the basis of equality, accepting it in terms of economic, cultural, and social change.

Acceptance offers much bigger trade-offs than the West Bank and Gaza. With the richness of the Arab, that trade-off cannot be excluded. In that great trade-off, we have acceptance and we have a regional set-up, for there is a great area of common regional interest between the Arabs and Israelis. We have agreement that the West Bank–Gaza area should not be penetrated by any foreign power, any subversive power, and both the Arabs and the Israelis have a share in that. The Arabs want the Palestinians to have a state, and Israel wants to be integrated in the area. This is a big trade-off in which we should invest. On the basis of these two interests, we can build a new, more integrated Middle East, not in the terms of unification of the past, but a unification and integration that accepts the uniqueness of every Arab country and of Israel. We need internal unification. It must be a gradual and sophisticated unification like the Economic Community in Europe.

The Middle East must evolve its own unification while respecting the uniqueness of each country and of each people in the area. In the long term, we have different problems. We must have popular acceptance. That goes far beyond the limitation of power. It includes not simply a tolerance of peace, but also acceptance on a religious, ideological level, an emotional level, a psychological level. It creates people-to-people interest. Some of the Israelis do not understand why an Egyptian finds it difficult to visit Israel and not be able to go to the West Bank, where his brother, the Palestinian, is under occupation. We understand the Israelis' mistrust of the Soviet Union when the Soviets discriminate against the Soviet Jews.

Above all, we must build a vested interest in peace, both on the political level and on the people level. In the long term, self-interest is the best guarantee for peace. In this process and in the prospects to come, there is a role for the European Economic Community, for Europe at large, for the United Nations, and for the Soviet Union if it wants to earn that right by supporting the ongoing process of cooperative peace in the area. The most important factor is structural change that increases the cost of war and rewards peace, based on a new constituency of Arabs and Israelis who believe in that change.

The Americans also must understand that they face a dilemma. In the past, American governments faced the Arab-Israeli problem but with great attention and sensitivity to the pro-Israeli constituency in America. The pro-Israeli constituency tended to outweigh all the interests of the Arabs and of America in the Arab world. But today we have a different scenario. The pro-Israeli constituency has shown great interest in real peace as championed by Sadat. The problem of choosing between the Israelis and the Arabs has been obviated.

America's security and its economic interests can be achieved by the solution of the Arab-Israeli conflict and not by the opposite. Those who are interested in and sensitive to the security of the area must understand that the security of the Middle East is complex. The Arab–Israeli conflict is one of many conflicts, although it is the most important. If all other regional conflicts are solved, this problem unresolved will tend to mar any reconciliation. Thus, any move toward security must start with security from within in order to gain security from without. No one can ignore that factor.

In conclusion, let me say that I see peace as a structural, revolutionary change, in the real terms of revolution. It is a change that influences people's concepts and motivations. It is multifaceted—economic, political, social, psychological. It must be based on the self-reliance of the parties, all the parties, but also on cooperation with those who want to support peace.

We must agree on the rules of the game, not one set of rules for the Israelis and another for the Arabs. If we do that, we must answer these questions: Who controls the people? After all the euphemisms and the diplomatic language, who controls the Palestinian people, and who controls their land and their resources? Unless the answer to these questions is that the Palestinian people should control their own destiny and control their land and their resources in peace, then this effort will not produce results. Timing is important, and security is important, but all must be done within an ongoing, unfolding process of peace.

I see in the Middle East two *D*s that need to be fulfilled—Deterence of any subversion outside or inside the region, and Development of the peace process by giving the Palestinians self-determination and economic, social, and political participation. With that image, we can see the peace process as much more challenging and as much more rewarding than is the diplomatic view of the peace process. Therein lies greater hope and greater risk. Thank you.

Questions and Answers

CHARLES SILLS, Martin-Marietta Aerospace: Mr. Ambassador, could you tell us specifically what your feelings and opinions are of the workability or inappropriateness of arms sales or arms transfers to the front-line or confrontation countries? This tool has been used in the past by the United States and by the Soviets and by other countries.

AMBASSADOR BASHEER: I personally would prefer that the front-line states—that is, Israel and the Arab states—in a state of war would have very few arms, because part of the peace process will be an attempt at demilitarization. We, in Egypt, are faced with the question of nuclear escalation by Israel and some Arab countries trying to catch up. We face this by ratifying the peace treaty. I am against the

16

United States giving Israel arms and not giving them to the Arab states. If the United States does not keep the balance that induces all the governments—Israel and the Arab states—to move to peace, then arms transfers should be limited. Arms should be given for the defense of the area collectively but within an atmosphere of specific, concrete advance to peace. The use of arms against the Palestinian people under occupation is illegal—contrary to what the Congress intended, contrary to what the world has accepted. The arms transfer policy must be seen as an element and tool of the peace process and not separate and different from it.

HAROLD SAUNDERS, American Enterprise Institute: You have in several ways indicated the importance of some dramatic gesture of acceptance of the existence of Israel by the Arab side. Sadat's visit to Jerusalem was such a gesture, and you have mentioned several other reasons why that was important. Is there a possibility of some comparable dramatization on the eastern side of Israel, on the Palestinian side of the acceptance of Israel, some dramatization that the structural change in thinking about the Middle East has taken place?

AMBASSADOR BASHEER: I believe that dramatization was a very important tool when it represented a real policy. I do not like dramatization when it becomes an empty gesture. The Sadat dramatization was enacted by Sadat going to Jerusalem. That was the real change. Israel has not answered that real dramatization by, in theory, accepting the right of the Palestinians in peace to self-determination. To come and ask those who are under occupation to recognize their occupiers as legitimate is asking the impossible. We do not have any example in past human history when the occupier was recognized as legitimate by the occupied. If Israel puts the Palestinians to the test by saying we are willing to sit with you, to negotiate a mutual recognition, in peace, between the Palestinians and the Israelis, then Israel can dramatize its commitment to peace, and the burden of proof will shift from the Israelis to the Palestinians. That is how you can move ahead, but to ask an occupied people to recognize its occupier is asking the impossible.

MR. SAUNDERS: I asked the question as one of the people who had been caught in the middle of this process of having each side tell us that if the other side would just move first, everything would be okay. You indicated earlier that that was one of the games both sides have played over the years. I am not so worried about who does it first, I am interested in the structure of making it happen. You have talked about how you can make it happen in Israel by encouraging one constituency for peace within Israel, and that process has begun. I am interested in how one can develop that constituency, that structural change, that change of mind on the Palestinian and Arab side, leaving aside for the moment the tactics of who ultimately goes first.

AMBASSADOR BASHEER: First of all, I do not take one constituency in Israel as the key. One constituency is symbolic of the trend toward peace, but peace means that all the constituencies, even the most extreme, must moderate their positions. You need a cross-mobilization of all constituencies, Arab and Israeli. One of the techniques of achieving the end you want is a meeting, under whatever sponsorship, to call for the Israelis and the Palestinians to negotiate mutual self-recognition. You bring them both the table, and you hope both will drink the water and work together. Those who do not play the game will be pinpointed and discovered, but you must give them some degree of symmetry in this recognition.

Egypt has already carried the burden, borne the cross, of recognizing, of making peace, of attending to Israeli sensibilities. Now, someone has to do that for the Palestinians, and what we are suggesting is that both they and the Israelis do it together. Third parties will have to make a conference in which they meet to understand each other and recognize each other mutually. If you wait for one side to do it, you are not going to have an easy repetition of the Sadat process. The Sadat process is by its very definition unique. What you can do, however, is use this process to bring them together and to make it impossible for either side not to recognize the other.

JERRY GREEN, Seven Springs Center: On this point of bringing people together, part of the problem is which Palestinians. I would be surprised, I would hardly expect Yassir Arafat and the leadership of the PLO voluntarily to abdicate the mantle that was cast upon them by the other Arab states—at least in Rabat, if not by the Palestinian people—as the sole spokesman for the Palestinian people. I am personally suspicious of that in the long run. I would hope that the Palestinians, not just in the West Bank and Gaza, but in the Palestinian Diaspora, could at some point—and you alluded to this, but not conclusively, in your remarks, at least I did not hear a conclusion—find others than the PLO to represent them in the kind of meeting you are talking about.

Another kind of step that might be taken in that context, which might make it easier for the other side to sit down, to find a way to meet somewhere and talk about it, would be to amend the Palestine

18

National Covenant to remove that difficult language about the structure of the state of Israel. I can envisage that it might be easier for those in Israel—and they have a problem of constituency as well—to engage in the kind of dialogue you described if the other side were represented, not by the PLO, but by somebody who had specifically rejected that part of the Palestine National Covenant. Do you see any prospect of that happening on the Arab side?

AMBASSADOR BASHEER: You have enumerated certain ideological concepts of the Palestinians, but you have not enumerated those of Israel and official statements of the government of Israel that are real threats to peace. If we start with this, we will never make peace. We can make peace despite the ideological underpinnings, because we have done it and we have proved it is possible. Why not call their bluff? If the PLO does not come to that meeting, then it will expose itself. If it comes, well and fine. It will be taking the risk of peace, making a reasonable calculated risk. Let us test them. I feel that the majority of the Palestinians in the PLO might take that challenge positively, but I cannot answer for them. We must offer them the challenge and wait for what happens. I also offer the challenge to the Israelis to see what they will do.

MORTON KONDRACKE, *The New Republic*: To carry that one step further, the argument against dealing with the PLO or acceding to Palestinian demands for self-determination is that inevitably a Palestinian state would be run by the PLO. The PLO has developed a close alliance with the Arab radical movement and with the Soviet Union, so inevitably this Palestinian state would be allied with the Soviet Union and would be radical and disruptive and a threat to its Arab neighbors, as well as to Israel. Is there a flaw in that logic? In other words, it is not merely rhetoric, it is interest and it is a habit of alliance that retards this. Is that somehow wrong?

AMBASSADOR BASHEER: Yes, it is wrong because it covers and blurs the issue. First, if some people are worried about the PLO, why were the people of the West Bank and Gaza not given full autonomy under Israeli military security? They do not have even the right to dig a well without permission. They cannot have political rights. They do not have industry. Their land is taken from them. Settlements are built. And you talk about the PLO. Why not give the people on the West Bank and Gaza full rights and see how much moderation that will produce?

Second, when the PLO started, it was a rightest movement. It came out of the Islamic position, not out of the leftist tradition. Moscow took a lot of years to recognize the PLO, but, like whatever is offered in any political game, Moscow offered a hand and the United States closed its doors and did not give visas. The PLO is essentially the main thrust, but it has many movements within it; it has a lot of contradiction, as the Zionist movement had in 1947. If the Palestinians have a country, if they have self-determination, I feel that the moderates will outweigh all extremists. But the way to settle this is by putting them to the test.

They are people who like their land; they are farmers. There is now a whole new bourgeoisie in the Middle East, and they take part in that. That means they will have a real interest in building. You push them and ignore them, then, as you say, they go to the Soviets. I can argue that they have not gone to the Soviet Union enough. They have been resisting radicalization. The question in any complex problem is how to have the mainstream moderate, but to have always some margins—the right or the left—who will say, "No, that is a treason." But it is the mainstream that makes history in the long run.

BEN WATTENBERG, American Enterprise Institute: Mr. Ambassador, Israel and the United States seem to be interested in exploring the idea of an American military presence in the Sinai when it reverts to Egypt under the final stage of the Camp David accords. Is that a plausible situation from the Egyptian point of view, particularly if it might be designed in such a way as to be coupled with greater Israeli accommodation in the autonomy talks?

AMBASSADOR BASHEER: That offer by Israel was not given to us, so I do not know where you got that. Israel has not offered to accommodate to the Palestinians in autonomy talks in exchange for a base in Sinai, and I do not know whom the base is for—the Israelis? After all, we negotiated the withdrawal of the Israelis from Sinai.

MR. WATTENBERG: The plan was for Americans to be in those air bases.

AMBASSADOR BASHEER: Israel is interested and also America; I will discuss America in a little while. Israel is interested in a base. Then it is welcome to offer America whatever number of bases Israel wants to offer America anywhere in Israel. We will not be against that. We leave the Israeli–American relationship to Israel and America.

We are very interested in the defense of the area, and when it

20

comes to that defense, particularly from Soviet or external threats, the Egyptians should have something to say. After all, we are the ones who had Soviets in a magnitude unprecedented in other countries, and we are the ones who got rid of the Soviets without American support—army, State Department, or CIA. At the time, the army and the CIA and the White House thought that Egypt could never overcome this. So if you want the defense of the area, we are very strongly willing to consult about the defense of the area. We asked Presidents Nixon, Ford, and Carter, and we will ask President Reagan about the defense of the area, not just in the Persian Gulf but also in Africa and on the Horn. For the past four presidents, our demands for defense of the area have not been met. In answer to your question, the new administration, when they come and visit— we will welcome Secretary Haig in a few days in Cairo—we will give them our opinion about how best to defend the Middle East.

We do not want to repeat your mistakes in Iran. After all, you talk about the defense of the area, after one of the greatest flukes in modern history, a defense of one of the rich allies that participated very strongly with it, and you could not keep the alliance. So you need to listen to us in close consultation on how to do it. We do not think bases will do it, but we have a whole measure of cooperation that we will ask of the American government. That proposal will be more effective in creating a defense of our area, both from within and from without, but I cannot discuss that here. I think Mr. Haig will hear some of it when he goes to Cairo.

JERRY HYMAN, American Enterprise Institute: Mr. Ambassador, you castigated to some extent the superpowers for not proposing a global solution but looking to the process of negotiation itself. I wonder, first, whether you see anything that the United States could do next in the peace process. What tangible moves could the United States specifically make? Second, given the outline you made about a real solution, which contains three elements—each party accepting the other as the other sees itself, none violating the minimum concerns of the other, and both avoiding the perception of threat— could you address yourself in some global way to a Palestinian solution? A Palestinian state would seem to violate at least two of those three conditions from the Israeli point of view—namely, it would be a threat and it would not meet the minimum concerns of Israel with regard to its own security.

AMBASSADOR BASHEER: First of all, I did not castigate the superpowers. I said they are impotent, they are unable to do it. I think the superpowers have a duty to help with it, but they must realize their limitations. Superpowers sometimes talk like small powers. We also make the same mistake, thinking that we have all the power. After all, there have been a lot of limitations in the role of the superpowers, whether it is the Russians or the Americans. But the superpowers and the third parties in general are a genuinely important, crucial element in helping the people oil the process and come together and make the process effective.

Now we will talk about people's perceptions. I do not think when Israel accepted to be a state, it accepted a Palestinian state. The Israelis accepted in 1947 an Arab state and a Jewish state with a common market, and that is the rule of the game. Within that general rule, I do not take maneuver tactics as perception. If the Israelis are afraid of a Palestinian state, then they can suggest a demilitarized state, because the Israelis also have not accepted to be the occupiers ad infinitum of the West Bank and Gaza. No one accepts anyone to be an occupier and still wants to be normal and friendly and a neighbor.

What I want is a process of bringing these two peoples together over time to recognize each other as people, as people who have political rights, and to negotiate in terms that will not threaten that either one will attack the other. Of course, in that case it would be the Palestinians, not doing what I see as guerrilla warfare, as against the fantastic ability of the Israeli army to attack at random and occupy all of Palestine and Lebanon and parts of Syria. It is in negotiation that these people can discover together how to come to real terms.

In many ways, we find negotiating with some Israelis easy because in the final analysis, it is the Israelis, the Palestinians, the Arabs, who will live and die in that area and who have a real interest in coming to peace. No one in the silent majority wants to live for a historical hatred and acrimony and unlimited war. It is on this axis that I hope negotiation will be fruitful, but this part is being attempted by superpowers.

You cannot signify the American role as a bystander, when it pays $2 or $3 billion to Israel or to Egypt, and gives them arms, and gives them technology. America is a partner in the peace process, and we want America to continue with that, but continuing it does not negate the self-reliance of the parties themselves to take courageous steps and to try to help each other heal the world.

GEORGE ASSOUSA, Carnegie Endowment for International Peace: Mr. Ambassador, I sense a lot of the questions that you were having to answer have implied connection between the continued possibility of further radicalization in the area and the connection with the Soviet Union. I wonder if you cannot excuse us for that in a sense. It is not, indeed, the Palestinian problem that is causing the increased presence of the Soviets in the Middle East. The need for doing that is what might lead us to a reduction of the threat of the Soviet Union.

Second, you have been here and have observed the administration and you have watched Mr. Sadat move into Europe recently. What are your thoughts as to a possible next move that would help bring Egypt closer to your initiative in the next stage?

AMBASSADOR BASHEER: Your first question regarding the Soviet Union would need a treatise on how a superpower behaves. A superpower calculus is dependent on many factors, but the existence of a major gap in the Middle East, which is the Arab–Israeli conflict, offers the best opportunity to be exploited by any inimical force. We want to bridge that gap so as not to give the Soviet Union or anybody a chance to exploit it.

America has been an asset compared to the Soviet Union so far in this project because America has worked as a healer while the Soviet Union has benefited from the maintenance of the status quo. The power of America as a healer is very important in this. The fact that the American consensus is somewhere between the Israeli consensus and the peace consensus helps America tremendously. The Soviet Union has not so far stated any real interest in having a genuine peace. When they do, we will welcome them.

As for your second question about Europe, President Sadat in his speech before the European Parliament in Luxembourg supported and encouraged the Europeans to come in and help with the process, to help in a way congenial with the process. In fact, in this problem we will need a lot of help, and the European role is much awaited. Europe should come and help the American efforts to push us ahead. One should not use this problem as a monopoly. America has the major role, but the European role is a very fruitful and effective one.

JOHN COOLEY, Carnegie Endowment for International Peace: Following up on your suggestion that structural changes are needed to bring about peace, I have two questions. From your observation of things, do you see any progress inside the Palestinian movement or in the Arab forces that exert influence on the Palestinians toward President Sadat's suggestion that they form a government in exile? The Algerians did this successfully and overcame many of the partisan difficulties they were having in the movement and in negotiating with the French. Second, it has been suggested in the recent past and also in the more distant past that the United Nations or some other supernational body organize an international consultation of all Palestinians to indicate their own feelings and wishes about the future and the future shape of their relations in peace with Israel and Jordan and their other neighbors and about the type of their entity. Where is that idea going, if anywhere?

AMBASSADOR BASHEER: About the government in exile, there is some such thought in the Arab position, but it has not been formulated in offering and choosing alternatives. Many are suspicious, but that did not prevent Iraq's asking Egypt for ammunition despite its rejection of Camp David. There is a contradiction in the Arab rejectionists' opposition because the so-called Arab rejection front is composed of two groups—moderate groups and people who are not as moderate.

On the second problem, the consultation, since 1917 the Palestinians have been subject to one committee of inquiry after another, to one wide book after another, to one U.S. committee after another. New consultation will not be fruitless if Israel is willing to pay more attention to that consultation. If the U.N. can devise some method of self-determination for the Palestinians, I think that might be fruitful. Two questions have to be answered by Israel—Who will control the Palestinians as people? Who will control their resources? When these questions have been answered, bets on peace should become higher.

MS. KIPPER: This is obviously a subject that we need to consider often and at length. We want to thank Ambassador Basheer and our questioners. I look forward to welcoming you all again to future sessions.

A Conversation with Ambassador Tahseen Basheer: Reflections o
the Middle East Peace Process is an edited transcript of a discussio
with Egypt's ambassador-designate to Canada. Ambassador Basheer'
candid discussion of the Camp David process includes the followin
comments:

*"I see peace as a structural, revolutionary change in the real terms of revc
lution. It is a change that influences people's concepts and motivations."*

*"Camp David is a process capable of development, modification, additior
and change. . . . All the parties, including the Palestinian people, must full
participate in the final settlement. . . . The cost of keeping the now-changec
unsettled status quo is very expensive."*

*"Egypt has been the innovator of peace, but Egypt cannot offer bridges (
acceptance to Israel. . . . The Arabs want the Palestinians to have a state
and Israel wants to be integrated in the area. . . . On the basis of these tw
interests, we can build a new, more integrated Middle East."*

Joining in the discussion are the scholars and guests of the America
Enterprise Institute.

ISBN 0–8447–3469–1

American Enterprise Institute for Public Policy Research
1150 Seventeenth Street, N.W., Washington, D.C. 20036